£2.00

D0708052

bailey
boat cat

bailey boat cat

ADVENTURES OF A FELINE AFLOAT

Louise Kennedy

ADLARD COLES NAUTICAL

B L O O M S B U R Y

LONDON · NEW DELHI · NEW YORK · SYDNEY

Published by Adlard Coles Nautical
an imprint of Bloomsbury Publishing Plc
50 Bedford Square, London WC1B 3DP
www.adlardcoles.com

Copyright © Louise Kennedy 2014

First published by
Adlard Coles Nautical in 2014

ISBN 978-1-4729-0650-2
ePDF 978-1-4729-0651-9
ePub 978-1-4729-0652-6

All rights reserved. No part of this publication may be reproduced in
any form or by any means – graphic, electronic or mechanical, including
photocopying, recording, taping or information storage and retrieval
systems – without the prior permission in writing of the publishers.

The right of the author to be identified as the author of this work
has been asserted by her in accordance with the Copyright,
Designs and Patents Act, 1988.

A CIP catalogue record for this book is available from the British Library.

This book is produced using paper that is made from wood grown in
managed, sustainable forests. It is natural, renewable and recyclable.
The logging and manufacturing processes conform to
the environmental regulations of the country of origin.

All photographs © Louise Kennedy
Design by Kevin Knight
Commissioned by Jessica Cole

Printed and bound in China by C&C Offset Printing Co

Note: while all reasonable care has been taken in the publication
of this book, the publisher takes no responsibility for the use
of the methods or products described in the book.

10 9 8 7 6 5 4 3 2

Contents

Hi furiends!

It's my pleasure to welcome you aboard! I'm a seal point Siamese who lives on a boat – and loves it! It may seem unusual to you that a cat would be so passionate about sailing but I'm sure that as you read my adventures, you'll understand why. And if you're not already an avid sailor, you'll soon want to be! There's nothing better than being out at sea on a glorious day – the wind billowing through your fur; the delicious fishy smell and the salty taste of the air swimming through your senses; dazzling sunsets on a panoramic horizon that make you dare to believe anything is possible.

I look after two humans who, although enthusiastic, need constant supervision! My beautiful boat is called *Nocturne* – affectionately known as *Noccy*. She's a Tayana 37, a true blue-water cruiser, and I love her more than anything in the world (except perhaps cat treats)!

Bailey
X X

6

Sailing skills

This looks like Treasure Island - there must be treats galore here!

Navigating... the Bailey way

I love finding our route using the charts with all the pretty symbols. I don't know why the humans spend so long looking at them – it's simple really...

1. Look at the chart.
2. Sail on the white bit.
3. Anchor in the blue bit.
4. Keep clear of the green bit.
5. Buy treats in the brown and yellow areas!

Move over, humans - I'll
show you how it's done!

Rules of the road

This is how all of the boats at sea avoid colliding with each other. The fact the humans call them 'rules of the road' when we're not even on land gives you an idea of how much help they need… so I have to supervise them at all times. Humans can be so slow sometimes! I can tell by a quick wiggle of my whiskers if there's a risk of collision, but I let the humans get involved too. I've taught them how to read the compass and check for transits.

The rules of the road tell all us sailors who gets to go first. The vessels with no one aboard take top priority – everyone else has to navigate around them. Next in line are the big boats – you know, the ones you wouldn't want to start a claw fight with. Then it's the fishermen – those guys have a pawesome job so we let them go ahead of us! Sailors come next (that's us) and finally it's the motorboats.

I'm trying to get them to make an official exception for vessels carrying a boat cat. Well, it's worth a try…

GPS (Getting Places Safely)

 Cats are very lucky to have an inbuilt sense of direction. We can find our way around very easily and it makes me giggle that my humans can be so clueless! Luckily for them, some slightly more intelligent humans invented a piece of equipment to help them figure out where they are. They call it a Global Positioning System, but I'll let you in on a secret… The real meaning of GPS is Getting Places Safely. It's a foolproof system to show them exactly where we are and help them remain calm.

I must admit, I do quite like the feature that tells us how fast we're going.

Reliable rigging

I regularly check the rigging. The rigging is what supports and controls the sails so it's very impawtant. I assess and examine every last paw place. It's essential that it's all in good working order so we can sail without any mishaps. It's a big job but someone has to do it!

Using the wind

When the sails catch the wind, the feeling is pawesome! My favourite point of sail is a beam reach because we go really fast! I love running downwind too, because it gives my fur a fabulous blow through. I always keep an eye on the humans though, because if the wind shifts, the boom (that's the pole along the bottom of the sail) might whack them on the head! Using the sails seems technical, but it's all about learning your boat and feeling the wind through your whiskers.

Trimming the sails

Trimming the sails is an art form. The smallest tweak can change the entire dynamic when we're out sailing. I like to think of the sails as wings: when they're set correctly, it really does feel as if we're flying. Since I spend so much of my time watching the seabirds, I consider myself something of an expert when it comes to wings and, therefore, sails.

I like to give the humans a sense of responsibility so I let them hoist the main and unfurl the foresail. But it's me who directs them on how to set and trim the sails!

Looking good - just need to pull the jammer down and the sails are set

My five steps to anchoring purrfectly

Wherever I drop my anchor, that's my home. The anchor is arguably the most impawtant piece of equipment you can have on a boat. If there's an emergency, you can use it to stop the boat drifting and running aground. Anchoring is also an impawtant skill if you enjoy cruising from one bay to another like I do!

1 PICK A PROTECTED ANCHORAGE
Always keep a paw on the weather forecast and choose a protected anchorage. That way, if bad weather strikes, you won't get your whiskers in a twist.

2 TAKE YOUR TIME
There's no rush. Make sure you're far enough away from any rocks or neighbouring boats. In the daylight it's much easier to choose the purrfect sandy spot.

3 ANCHOR!

Lower the anchor a little and let it settle in while you admire your new home. Then slowly put out more chain and let the wind, the tide and the boat do their jobs. I purr at *Nocturne* to guide her gently if she needs help. You can usually feel when the anchor bites, which is very reassuring. I make my humans mark the chain, too, so I can supervise how much we let out.

4 ANCHOR ALARM

Pick out some landmarks along the shore so you can easily identify if you're drifting. I'm really good at this, but the humans also plot their coordinates on the GPS. It sets off an alarm to alert them if the boat starts to drag. No one wants to be woken up from a cat nap because the boat has hit something!

5 WAIT

After anchoring you should always stay on board for long enough to ensure that the boat is holding well. We normally wait for at least an hour before venturing out in the dinghy. I like to take this opportunity to eat some treats!

WHISKER  WISDOM

Take a look around:
life is pawesome!

Five knots
every boat cat should know

1 CLOVE HITCH Used to hang up toy mice quickly and easily.

2 REEF KNOT Used to join rope together so I can dangle bait overboard and attract the fish.

3 ROUND TURN AND TWO HALF HITCHES Attach around a human to keep them on a lead.

4 BOWLINE Makes a secure loop so I can lasso my treats and pull them towards me!

5 BAILEY'S KNOT This one's purely for fun!

Safety at sea

Lifejackets

Since I'm a cat, not only am I above the rules, but generally it's me that makes the rules! When it comes to safety, however, you can never be too careful. So if the conditions at sea are anything but purrfect I insist that we all wear our lifejackets. They really do look silly but safety comes first!

Truth be told, I mostly wear mine to make the clumsy bipeds feel better - I've got four paws, agility and balance a ninja would be proud of!

Cat overboard!

One situation every sailor dreads is a man-overboard emergency. I've made my crew do lots of man-overboard drills, so they're prepared if it ever happens. Then one day they suggested a cat-overboard drill. My poor naive humans were genuinely concerned that I might fall overboard while they're ashore getting provisions. How ridiculous! I watched with interest as they made a rope ladder for me. It's actually rather charming that the humans feel they have to look after me. We all know it's me who looks after them!

I very rarely go for a swim because of the fur grooming involved afterwards. But since they were so insistent, I decided to humour them. They showed me their rope-ladder creation from the dinghy and offered words of encouragement.

They were keen for me to climb straight up the ladder but since I was getting wet, I decided to do a couple of laps of the boat. They took this to mean I had misunderstood. Purr-lease! When one of them got in to 'help' me, I decided enough was enough and climbed right up the ladder!

Climb up that ladder? I thought you said you had a challenge for me!

For any other felines who fancy a swim in the ocean, I recommend it! But be sure to have a freshwater shower before attending to your furstyle.

Salty furballs are NEVER fun.

Seasickness

Any sailor worth their salt will tell you everyone suffers from seasickness at one time or another. There's no shame in it. The ocean is powerful and sometimes it can make your tummy flip. Of my two humans, one is very prone to it, while the other one rarely suffers. The best thing is to try to prevent it rather than cure it. Here are my top prevention tips!

- Eat well before sailing. I purrsonally enjoy a meat-flavoured biscuit.
- Stay hydrated. Remember: we're sailors, water is our friend!
- Stay in the shade to avoid getting dehydrated.

The first signs of seasickness are very subtle. You might feel breathless or drowsy, and most people feel sick. In some cases, actually being sick can follow, which is very unpleasant. I warn my humans when I'm about to be sick by licking my lips a lot. I've also learnt to make sure the humans lean the right way when they need to be sick, after a rather unglamorous incident!

When we're feeling bad, being in the fresh air usually helps. I curl up in my travel box and let the breeze ruffle my whiskers. Snacking on dried food helps, too. And, if it's really that bad, I like to sleep it off. A cat nap is ALWAYS welcome!

Meowww! Feeling under paw - time for a cat nap!

Meowday! Meowday!

If you and your boat are in grave danger, it may be necessary to make a Meowday message. It goes something like this:

MEOWDAY MAYDAY MEOWDAY

This is: *Nocturne Nocturne Nocturne*

MEOWDAY

I require immediate assistance.

My position is 100 paw prints away from the lighthouse with the fun light beam.

We have hit a rock and are taking on water.

I have 2 humans on board.

We are trying to plug the hole.

Nocturne

OVER

Boat-cat survival kit

I hope I'll never need it but I do have a boat-cat survival kit on board, just in case. It's pretty down to earth – bandages, tape, cleansing wipes, special eye wash, and a foil wrap, to name just a few items. The humans can't be trusted to check it, so I carry out my own inspections.

Clumsy creatures

Some people think sailing is dangerous. Seriously, it's one of the world's safest pastimes as long as you've got some common sense – or a cat to look after you! Humans are naturally clumsy but I'm a fearless feline. I've had to rig a preventer on board, though, to stop the humans getting hit on the head by the boom. They look surprised every time it happens!

Fire in the hold

Fire prevention is essential on a boat. You need to be especially careful when you're cooking. Make sure you know where the fire extinguishers and fire blanket are, just in case you do hiss it up and cause a fire. Obviously, singed fur and withered whiskers would be cat-astrophic!

Is it me, or is it getting hot in here?

Pyrotechnics

With my expertise, this boat should never sink, but I've made sure we carry flares on board just in case there is an emergency. For an emergency at night, we have a flare gun – the flares look like fireworks! If it's daytime, we've got orange smoke. Paw signals are the other way to show we're in distress. If anything happens, follow my lead.

WHISKER WISDOM

With a little patience and lots of positivity, anything is possible...

Bilge rats

The bilge is what we call the inside part of a boat that sits under the waterline. It's where we keep the pumps, which are another cool safety feature. If there's a leak, the automatic bilge pump will protect us. My humans nearly flooded the boat once because they forgot to turn off the hose when they filled the water tanks. I should never have trusted them to take care of it themselves! I check the pumps quite a lot because I like to go down into the bilge to patrol for bilge rats. I'm proud to say we've never had a problem, but I take my pest control seriously and investigate regularly.

Everything's in working order, but it could do with a clean

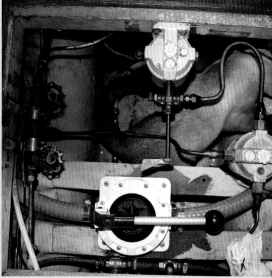

Fantastic fenders

As I'm sure you all know, we cats use our whiskers to judge if we can safely fit through something. Fenders are like whiskers for boats! Well, sort of. They're not exactly the same but not everything can be as cool as a cat! If the boat is too close to something, the inflatable fenders will cushion any contact and keep the boat safe and scratch-free. When we don't need them, I love lounging on them. They're also great to exercise on or hide behind.

Galley grub

Dinghy devils

On the top of my wish list for dinner every day are dinghy devils. Humans call them seagulls. Their mission in life is to take over the dinghy – they're like flying pirates! They thieve at every opportunity and drive me crazy with their cackling. I've even noticed the lazy dinghy devils hitchhiking. They stand there with their heads proudly thrust in the air as if they own my dinghy! And when I'm fishing they circle overhead, ready to swoop down and steal my delicious fish.

Just a little closer... come juuuust a little closer!

I really don't have anything nice to say about dinghy devils - except they might taste good... I just need to catch one to find out!

Fish are furiends

I bet you think that I eat fish every day, because I live on a boat. Well, I would if my humans could catch them. The rather embarrassing truth is that they're hopeless.

It doesn't take them hours, it takes them days! If they're lucky, they'll catch a tiny fish that's far too cute to eat. I have been known to turn my paw to fishing to show the humans how it's done.

Hey little fishy, would you like to stay for dinner?

WHISKER WISDOM

When you're hungry, eat.
When you're tired, take a nap.
When you crave adventure... go sailing.

Running the galley gauntlet

Cooking on a boat is very different from cooking on land. The main difference is we're moving! Our stove is gimballed: it's on two pivot points, allowing it to swing back and forth, so it stays level even when the boat isn't. It's also fun to jump on and practise my balance as it swings!

Ah! Hot, hot, hot!... only joking, it's switched off – I'm not stupid, you know!

Tempting treats

I make sure we all have treats readily available on board. I let the humans have some, so they don't feel left out. I love special treats that they don't like, which means I don't have to share! My treat ball is great fun. Luckily, in the cat world it's not impolite to play with your food!

Monster mosquitoes

In certain anchorages and marinas, mosquitos can cause havoc. Once I tried one because I thought the little bloodsucker would be juicy but the taste was disappointing. These nasty 'mozzies', as my humans call them, can spoil the evening. They buzz on board without so much as an invitation. It's amazing how something so small can create such a commotion. When the humans hear their high-pitched monster music, they start slapping themselves, clapping thin air and huffing and puffing. They even try to gas us all by spraying chemicals. It's really quite distressing! The only way to calm the humans down is to hunt the monster mosquitoes so we can all get a good night's sleep.

WHISKER WISDOM

Only a true sailor can be both
Relaxed and Ready for anything...

Eight ways to communicate with your tongue!

Well done crew, keep it up!

I am not amused.

Jellyfish alert!

Turn to the left a bit...

Human, you really do talk some nonsense.

I want to eat you, dinghy devils!

I spy dinner...

If you want a job done properly, you should do it yourself.

Come rain
or shine

Weather windows

 We spend a lot of time calculating weather windows and even more time waiting for them! A weather window is a period of time when the weather is suitable for making a passage. If you have good weather, a day's sailing can make you feel like you're on top of the world. If there are scary storms, it can make you wonder why you chose to be on a boat! I prefer to be snuggled up in a safe anchorage or a marina during bad weather. Our *Noccy* doesn't seem to mind at all. Sometimes I even think she prefers it when it's rough! She makes wild waves look like little ripples as she glides over them. It's quite reassuring to know that she's in her element when I'm curled up in my cabin.

Weather window says no.
Let's try again tomorrow.

Sir Rocco

One evening we were at anchor and the humans were getting very excited about someone called 'Sir Rocco' coming. They put everything away and tidied up the whole boat without me even telling them to! When they got the second anchor out I knew this guy must be someone impawtant.

That first night came and went with nothing to report. I presumed Sir Rocco was late. Then, on the second night, I thought that someone was really really angry – there was a huge howling sound coming from outside…

The next morning we woke up to a red dust all over the boat. It turns out that Sir Rocco isn't a human at all – he's a seriously strong wind that blows from the south. Never mind that, though: with the second anchor in use, its storage bag was free for me. It's purrfect to hide in!

Music to my furry ears

As much as I love basking in sun puddles on a glorious day, I must admit that I really enjoy the rain, too. When you are all cosy inside a boat, the rain is rather special. It makes a pawesome pitter-patter noise that's like music to my furry ears – it makes me dream of mice scurrying about! And I love watching the raindrops trickle down the glass.

WHISKER WISDOM

There is no better place on a hot day than the shade of a sail.

Blue-green

I'm often called Bailey-Blue thanks to my big blue eyes, but Bailey-Green might be a better name for me. I make sure we stay as green as possible on board *Nocturne* – we use a wind turbine and solar panels to generate energy on top of batteries. The wind turbine makes a funny whizzing noise, so I prefer the solar panels. They're purrfect for sleeping on, too.

Top five cloud calculations

1 If the clouds are black, low and look like a pack of dogs waiting to strike, you can expect a storm.

2 A greyish veil over the clouds means wet weather is on the way.

3 Cirrus clouds are the thin wispy ones. I think they are what a hiss would look like. As with any hiss, you should be wary and alert for a sudden change.

4 Cirrostratus clouds are thin, high clouds that cover the entire sky like a comfy blanket. They mean it's time to snuggle up in a box because the weather will be dull and drizzly.

5 Cumulonimbus clouds are the big, tall, menacing guys that contain lightning... If I see these monsters, I instruct the humans to stay put and feed me treats. Meowza! I don't want to be struck by lightning!

Dependable dinghy

Our dinghy is effectively our family car. Not only do we use it to get ashore while at anchor, but we also explore islands and go right into bays and caves in shallow water where we wouldn't be able to take *Nocturne*. To begin with, the humans were concerned that I'd make a hole in the dinghy with my claws. I can assure you that I would never be so silly. My claws are retractable; unfortunately, their strange ideas are not! It's me that should be concerned about the wellbeing of the dinghy when they go too close to the rocks!

Boat maintenance

Oily operations

We enjoy looking after *Nocturne* and giving her lots of TLC. Every year the engine oil needs to be changed and the filters replaced. It's quite a messy job! Luckily, the humans picked up some special mats that soak up spills and keep the floor clean. I can't even begin to imagine how long it would take to clean off oily paws. Not to mention how they'd taste! Urgh!

Well done, humans - you've passed the paw patrol this time

Clawing the ropes

On a boat, ropes are involved in nearly everything. They can be used for mooring, anchoring, towing and fastening. We use them for raising sails, trimming sails, sharpening my claws and countless other tasks. The ropes are really important, so they're always kept neatly coiled and stored off the ground.

WHISKER WISDOM

To be curious on a boat is to have the world at your paws.

Salty sails

We regularly check our sails for any signs of wear and tear. The UV rays in sunlight are very damaging, so we always put on protective sail covers. Occasionally the sails need a good wash to get rid of salt and dirt. Just like me, they're often reluctant to be hosed down, but oh my cat they look pawesome when they come out all sparkling and clean. I take sail inspections very seriously - especially if I can snuggle up in freshly laundered sail bags!

The smell of salty air is best enjoyed from the comfort of a sail

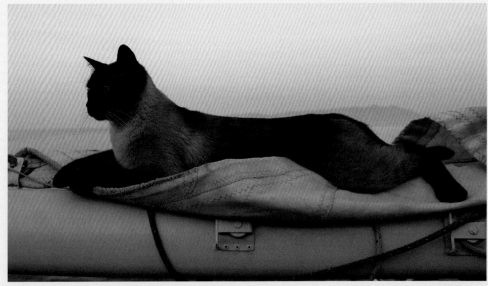

Sticky stuff

We have boxes and boxes full of sticky stuff on board to help with repairs. The humans go crazy for it. I think it's their equivalent of catnip. They call it epoxy and it sticks things together. Me, I can't see what all the fuss is about – give me catnip any day!

VHF (Very Happy Feline)

VHF is a special radio we use to call marinas and other boats, or to make a Meowday call. VHF stands for Very Happy Feline. When the humans are occupied chatting on the VHF, I can have a little break from supervising. I also like to call my furiends when they aren't looking!

Cable ties

After sails and ropes, cable ties are the most useful piece of equipment on a boat. We have hundreds of them in every colour and size you could think of. You can use them for almost everything. They keep cables neat, join things together and we can even fix equipment with them. But the very best thing about them is that they're great to play with!

WHISKER WISDOM

Face your fears ears forward, nose up, whiskers waiting.

Scrubbing the decks

We have to be careful to protect our beautiful *Noccy* from the sun, salt and stains so we regularly scrub the decks. I love supervising the scrubbing stage and often take control of hosing down to ensure I don't get wet! The hose seems to have a life of its own sometimes!

Top five things to remember
in an emergency

1 Put all your cat treats in the grab bag to take with you.

2 Make sure you're groomed and looking furry and fabulous for the rescue crew.

3 Take a trip to the litter box so you're ready for anything.

4 Take the opportunity to scratch all the furniture. You might not get the pleasure again.

5 Don't forget your toy mice, humans and any other valuables when you leave the boat.

Playtime on board

Six ways to keep fit on board

Some humans wonder how to stay fit and healthy when you live aboard. I think it's quite simple really. I have a small daily routine to make sure I stay in shape!

I do some pull ups

Followed by sideways stretches

Then I climb...

... so I can do the REVERSE hula around the foresail.

Next I do PRESS ups...

And finally, I make sure I fit in plenty of cardio exercise by RUNNING and jumping around the boat.

The humans are lazy in comparison but they do swim. I need to throw them in more often to keep them active, although they'll never be in such good shape as me!

Kayaking

One of the best toys we have on the boat is the inflatable kayak. It keeps the humans quiet for ages! They happily paddle off to explore and I get some peace and quiet. I was wary of such a big toy at first, but it actually takes up very little space when it's deflated. And it's versatile, too: it's comfy to lie on, and it makes a great shady spot on hot days.

Keeping cool
under the
kayak is a
great way to
beat the heat

No secrets

The humans use something they call the head to relieve themselves on the boat. I've never understood why it's called the head, since they use it for their tail-end. It's just a fancy litter tray that they pump water through until it's clean.

Since they're unable to groom themselves, they also have a shower. I've had the misfortune of having to use it after my swimming adventures. It does the job, I suppose, but grooming is so much more enjoyable.

I always remind the humans to wash their paws after using the head!

WHISKER WISDOM

To purr from within,
take the time to fix your fur.

Cubby holes

Noccy is the perfect location for a game of hide and seek because she's got so many cubby holes! I find it hilarious watching the humans look for me. When they really can't find me, they rattle my treats. Then I'll grace them with my presence… in exchange for something yummy!

Making new furiends

Living on the boat, we're very lucky to make lots of new furiends. One evening we saw the biggest, brightest shooting star. I made a wish and ten minutes later a flying fish dropped in to say hello! I couldn't believe my eyes. He was the most pawesome fish I have ever seen in my life! We also had a starfish pop in for a chat once.

My favourite furiends, however, don't come aboard. They swim along with us at the bow of the boat!

I love flying visits from the stars of the ocean!

Dolphins are my favourite furiends - they bring us luck when they swim with us

Cats vs. dogs

There is no doubt in my mind that I'm much more intelligent than any dog. Humans talk about man's best friend as though he's some kind of hero. He can sit and walk to heel at a single command. Excuse me, but that doesn't seem to be a sign of intelligence in my opinion. It's obedience, sure, but not intelligence!

When I'm in the mood, I can be very obedient. I often say please when I want a treat. I come running when my name is called. I understand that when my humans say NO, it's because they don't want me to do something or they want me to stop doing something... Like climbing up the sails, for example!

But even though I'm quite capable of obeying, I often decide not to. I'm independent, I know what I want and I know how to get it! I didn't get to be a boat cat by doing as I was told. I've proved to my humans on many occasions that I know best. Sometimes I let them think they've won, but we all know who really runs the show!

Dogs are cute, I'll give them that. I've even learned how to use their most powerful weapon myself. When I put on my 'puppy dog eyes' it's remarkably effective!

Don't get me wrong, I love dogs. But the simple fact is that cats (especially Siamese) make much better sailors!

Top five reasons to set sail

1 As a boat cat, I get plenty of attention wherever we go.

2 There are fish EVERYWHERE!

3 You make lifelong furiends - sailors and cruisers are a great bunch!

4 You're continuing a tradition that's more than 3000 years old. (I'm still working on bringing back the tradition of worshipping cats!)

5 Sailing is simply PAWESOME!

Paws for thought

I hope you've enjoyed discovering what life is like as a boat cat. But before I leave you, here is my closing whisker wisdom, for all the humans who long to sail…

I often hear humans complaining about being run down. How do they get into this state? I believe it's because most humans haven't got their 'work-life balance' anywhere near actually balancing. They need to relax and have a good stretch!

OK, so work is impawtant but don't forget who you are and what you love – and take the time to enjoy life! I am a boat cat and I love sailing. I take my writing work seriously but I think everyone should allow time for the things they love and the things that inspire them.

I've been training my humans to think like this. They're now taking more time to lead a healthy, sustainable lifestyle while we plan another adventure on our beautiful *Nocturne*.

You might think me unqualified for giving advice to humans, but just ask yourself this: when did you last see a worn-out cat?

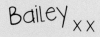

Bailey x x